Abdullah

Father of the Holy Prophet Muhammad

(Peace be upon him)

by

Riaz Hussain, M. A.

KITAB BHAVAN

New Delhi-110002 (INDIA)

KITAB BHAVAN
1784, Kalan Mahal, Darya Ganj,
New Delhi-1100 02
Phone : 91-11-23277392/93, 23274686
Fax : 91-11-23263383
Email : nasri@vsnl.com
Website : www.kitabbhavan.com

Edition 2005

ISBN : 81-7151-362-X

Laser Typesetting at :
T.J. Enterprises
Pataudi House, Darya Ganj,
New Delhi-1100 02 (India)

Published by :
Nusrat Ali Nasri for Kitab Bhavan
1784, Kalan Mahal, Darya Ganj,
New Delhi-1100 02 (India)

Printed in India at :
Lahooti Fine Art Press
1711, Suiwalan,
New Delhi-1100 02 (India)

CONTENTS

Publisher's Note

The Publisher humbly presents to the readers this biography of the Holy Prophet's august Father, the first world literature.

Preface

What kind of a man he was whose son was chosen by Allah to be His Last Prophet ?

Well, first and foremost, Abdullah the father of the Holy Prophet Muhammad (peace be upon him) was the descendant of three Prophets. He was a unique man among his contemporaries. He was content when men of his age were generally profligate. He practised a high degree of moral purity, Fornication, drinking, and dice were the common and socially accepted pastimes in his milieu. Yet, there is strong evidence that he kept aloof from them.

The people were devoted to gods made of wood and stone and other mundane materials, yet he clung to the creed of one God and was member of a tiny group of Unitarians called 'Hunafa'.

Among usurers, financial speculators, hoarders, exploiters and slave-drivers he held his place as a humble, honest trader in dates and spices.

He was loved by his father and brothers, adored by sisters and admired by the whole city whose populace called him 'The Lamp' He was coveted by beautiful women and sought after by powerful chiefs as a match for their daughters. These were the kinds of opportunities which his peers would instantly grasp, yet he chose to take in solemn marriage the daughter of a chief, not in the front rank of worldly power or pelf.

Ka'abah the House of Allah had long been turned by heathens into a house of many gods. For long had the fornicators, daughter-killers, gamblers and murderers ruled the land. Allah now willed that a man who had remained so steadfast to his creed and so pure in morals should be rewarded with a son who would in due time be commissioned as the Final Prophet (P.B.U.H.).

No independent work on the Life of Abdullah has yet appeared in any language of the world. The author's modest attempt, first as it is in the entire history of Islamic Literature of fourteen centuries, will, it is hoped, be favourably received.

I may add that the idea of this attempt first. occurred to me while I was assisting Late Professor Abdul Hameed Siddiqui in the English translation of the Holy Qur'an in the course of which I came across several verses lauding the hunafa, worshippors of one Allah even in the dark days of Ignorance.

It is also apt to record that through the courtosy of my esteemed friend Khan Abdul waheed Khan, Secretary and General Manager, Islamic Publications Ltd., Lahore, the contents of this work were briefly discussed with late Maulana Syed Abul Aa'la Maudoodi who suggested the title Abdullah, the Father of the Holy Prophet Muhammad (PBUH). The readers will please note, however, that any errors of commission or omission are solely mine.

Riaz Hussain

ANCESTRY

The Prophet Abraham (peace be on him) was the forebear of Abdullah, father of Muhammad (peace be upon him). Abraham's son was Ismael whose descen-dants founded various branches of the Quraish, the dominant trading tribe of Arabia, In the third generation of Abraham's family a person named Qaidar achieved great prominence. He was the second son of Ismael. In Hebrew the word 'Qaidar' denotes 'sombre' or 'dark'. Arabic Lexicon too contains the words 'Qadr' or 'Qadurat' meaning 'blackness' or 'Sombre mood'. Actually 'Qaidar' appears to have been an affectionate epithet conferred by Ismael upon his son, who was always absent from home on long journeys and thus caused the heartache of separation to his doting father. It is possible that the family gave the nickname Qaidar to the boy because" of his dark complexion or sombre mien.

The historical importance of Qaidar may be noted from the fact that he is mentioned in the pages of Torah, Assyrian tablets and ancient Greek histories.

Arian, Ptolemy and Pliny give clear evidence of the existence of Qaidari tribe in the Hijaz Province of

Arabia.[1] Yet another testimony to the greatness of Qaidar is provided by the fact that in recognition of his pre-eminent position the people began to call themselves Qaidari. As a nation, the Qaidaries are first mentioned in Prophet David's scripture Zabur (110 B.C.) At that age the Qaidaries lived in tents.

Zabur relates that the Prophet David had made a long stay with the Qaidari people in their tents.

(Zabur, 5—120)

The Prophet Suleiman in one of his Odes also describes the tents of the Qaidari people as of black colour and mentions 'I am dark as the dark tents of the Qaidaries.

These tents were made of dark quilt cloth, A few generations before Muhammad's (peace bo on him) time Makkah itself was a city of black tents with no stone or mud houses in existence.

Some generations later the next notable personage of the family is Adnan, who was the chief Lord of Arabia in his time. Eleventh in the line of descent from Adnan was Fahr, whose surname was Quraish. He was one of the prominent chiefs of Arabia and a leading merchant. His surname Quraish meant "Getter", "Recipient", "Earner". It was, therefore, because of

1. Forester, *'Arab Geography'* Vol. 1, p. 248.

his capacity to earn immense wealth that he came to be known as "Quraish". Since his tribe also mostly followed the vocation of trading so they were all collectively known as "Quraishis". The word Quraish also means a "gathering" an 'assembly' a society, but this also points to a "Guild of Traders". Abdullah bin Abbas states "Quraish is the name of an animal which inhabits the river. It preys upon lesser animals. Hence Fahr had adopted this surname to symbolise his power."

It might be noted that in ancient Arabia no animal called Quraish was ever worshipped. Hence we may be certain that Fahr had not added this word to his name because of any religious considerations.

Among the progeny of Fahr, the most renowned was Hashim. This gentleman is the nearest progenitor of Abdullah and it is after his name that the family of Muhammad (peace be on him) came to be known as Banu Hashim. Hashim was reputed to be an exceedingly handsome man and one who possessed a pure character. The men of Banu Hashim were known by one distinguishing mark *i.e.* their fore-heads were strikingly bright and luminous. The light that shone in Hashim's forehead especially elicited admiration of onlookers. The prestige of his family, personal beauty and accomplishments had made him the most eligible match in all Arabia and many Arab chiefs and scholars of the people of the Book (Jews and Christians) wanted to give their daughters in marriage to him. That, he held a commanding political authority in Arabia is attested by the fact that the Roman Emperor Heracles in pursuance of a policy to strengthen the Empire in the East, also desired to effect a matrimonial alliance between his daughter and Hashim, to whom he wrote a letter, saying, "The fame of your pure character has reached me, come to me and give me the honour of being my son-in-law.[1] Hashim thankfully declined all matrimonial proposals advanced by notable families of the, Jews and Christians of Arabia as also the offer sent by Emperor Heracles of Rome, He chose for his bride a beautiful lady, Salms daughter of Amar, from the tribe of Najjar She bore him Abdul Muttalib. From his childhood Abdul Muttalib was energetic and brave. He was Always active in public service. He had inherited from his forefathers a refulgence in the forehead. People knew him by a multitude of names, all of which testify to his power and eminence. His real name was Aamer.

As he was born with a clump of grey hair on the head, he was given the appellation "Shaiba" meaning 'advanced in years'. His most popular name is Abdul Muttalib. He had adopted this name in honour of his uncle Muttalib who had brought him up. Besides these

1. Aulad Haider Bilgrami.

the Quraish called him by such epithets as shabih al Hamd Fayaz[1], Muattam Tair al-Sama, Saqi al-Hejaz[2] Saqi al-Ghaith[3], Saqli Zam-Zam[4] and Sheriff Quraish.[5]

As mentioned earlier Abdul Muttalib earnestly engaged himself in public service and constantly thought of new plans for the welfare of wayfarers and pilgrims.

The memory of a well called Zam-Zam had long been preserved in the minds of Makkans, but no one knew where it had been originally located. Four hundred years before the time of Abdul Muttalib a certain Umro bin al-Harith was the Lord of Makkah—Apprehending an attack from his foes, Harith fled from Makkah and as a measure to deny water to the invaders filled the Zam-Zam with earth. Ali bin Abu Talib has related the story of the digging of Zam-Zam thus : Abdul Muttalib said "I was sleeping in the Hijr when a supernatural visitant came and said "Dig Tibba". I said, "And what is Tibba ?" Then he departed. Next day while I was asleep he came to me again and said "Dig Barra", when I enquired "what is Barra ?" he left me.

---

1. Praiseworthy, generous.
2. Host of Hejaz.
3. Host of Al-Ghaith.
4. Host of the Spring of Zam-Zam.
5. Is the honorific title indicating his position of leadership in Makkah.

On the third day he came and said, "Dig al-Madnuna", when I asked what that was he went away ngain. On the fourth day he appeared in my sleep again and said "Dig Zam-Zam". I asked "What is Zam-Zam ?" Abdul Muttalib constantly thought of reopening the well for enhancing the water supply for the use of the citizens of Makkah and the merchants and pilgrims who came from outside.

One day while Abdul Muttalib was sleeping in the Hijr (it is the semi circular spot between the wall called Hatim and the Ka'abah, which is said to contain the graves of Hagar and Ismael), he saw a dream in the course of which he was ordered to dig the zam-zam.

Whereupon he said : 'Twill never fail or ever run dry, 'Twill water the pilgrim company. It lies 'twixt the dung and the flesh bloody, By the nest where the white-winged ravens fly, By the nest where the ants to and fro do play".[1]

It may fairly be assumed that the sacrificial animals were tethered at a certain spot and there they would void ordure before they were led to the foot of the image at which they were slaughtered. A point between

1. Ibn-i-Tshaque, Sirat Rasul Allah, trans. A, Guillaum (Oxford University Press, Karachi. 1955), pp 62-68.

these two spots was more closely defined by the ants and the raven's nest, which must have already been known to Abdul Muttalib during his daily round of the Ka'abah.

Now when the exact spot had been indicated to him and he knew that it corresponded with the facts, he took a pickaxe and went with his son al-Harith — for he had no other son at that time — and began to dig. When the top of the well appeared he cried. "Allaho Akbar". Thus Quraish knew that he had obtained his object and they came to him and raised a quarrel saying, "This is the well of our father Ismael, and we have a right to it, so give us a share in it". "I will not", he answered, "Its site was indicated to me only and I therefore hold title to it." They said "Do us justice. We shall not leave you until we have got a judicial decision in the matter." He said' "Appoint anyone you like as umpire between us." He agreeed to accept a woman divine of B. Sa'd Hudhaym, who dwelt in the uplands of Syria. So 'Abdul Muttalib, accompanied by his relations and representatives of all the tribes of Quraish, rode away. They went on through desolate country between the Hijaz and Syria until Abdul Muttalib's company ran out of water and they feared that they would die of thirst. They asked the Quraish tribes to give them water but they refused on the pretext that if they gave them their water they too would die of thirst.

In his desperation Abdul Muttalib consulted his companion as to what would be done, but all they could do was to say that they would follow his instructions. So he said, "I think that every man should dig a hole for himself with the strength that he has left so that whenever a man dies his companions can thrust him into the hole and bury him until the last man for it is better that one man should be unburied than a whole company". They accepted his advice and every man began to dig a hole for himself. Then they sat down until they should die of thirst. After a time Abdul Muttalib said to his companions, By Allah to abandon ourselves to death in this way and not to scour the country in search of water is sheer incompetence. Perhaps Allah will give us water somewhere. "To your sadles." So they got their beasts ready while the Quraish watched them at work. Abdul Muttalib went to his beast and mounted her and when she got up from her knees a flow of fresh water broke out from beneath her feet. Abdul Muttalib and his companions crying "Allah-o-Akbar" dismounted and drank and filled their water skins. Then they invited the Quraish to come to the water which Allah had given them and to drink freely. After they had done so and filled their water skins they said, "By Allah, the judgment has been given in your favour, Abdul Muttalib. We will never dispute your claim to Zam Zam. He Who has given you water in this wilderness is He Who has given you Zam Zam, Return to your office of watering the pilgrims in peace". So they all went back without going to the diviner.

Yazid bin Abu Habib al-Misri on the authority of Abdullah bin Zurayr-al-Ghafiqi reports that Abdul Muttalib himself related the incident thus : "When I was ordered to dig Zam Zam it was said to me :

Then pray for much water as crystal clear.
To water Allah pilgrims at the sites they revere
As long as it lasts you have nothing to fear.

On hearing these words I went to the Quraish and said, "you know that I have been ordered to dig Zam-Zam for you", and they asked, ' But have you been told where it is?" When I replied that I had not been told, they asked me to go back to my bed where I had the vision and if it really came from Allah it would be made plain to me; but if it had come from a demon, he would not return to me. So I went back to my bed and slept and received the following message :

Dlg Zam-Zam, 'twill not to your hopes givc lie,
'Tis yours from your father eternally.
'Twill never fail or even run dry,
'Twill water the pilgrim company
Like on ostrich flocks a fraternity,

Their voice Allah hears most graciously.

A pact most sure from days gone by Nought like it canst thou descry,

It lies twixt the dung and the flesh bloody.[1]

From Zam Zam Abdul Muttalib supplied the pilgrims ; and the water itself soon began to share in the sacredness of the Ka'abah and its rites. The fame and influence of Abdul Muttalib now began to wax greater and greater, a large family of powerful sons added to his dignity ; he became, and continued to his death, the virtual chief of Makkah. (Sprenger considers that the Omeyed family had the preeminence. It is certain that Harb, and after him Abu Sofyan, surpassed the family of Hashim in wealth and influence and that they were the chiefs of Makkah).[2]

However Muir believes that Abdul Muttalib was the virtual chief of Makkah. After his death there existed an equality among the several families ; there was no real chief over the whole city.

> "Sheba al-Hamd, the same is Abdul Muttalib, was the Chief of the Coreish until his death".[3]

---

1. Ibn-i-Ishaque Op Cit., pp. 62-68.
2. Sprenger p, 31.
3. *Kitab al-Wagidip.* 14 as tra nslated by William Muir, *Life of Mohmet,* pp. CCiVII/CCiVIII.

A strange calamity threatened to embitter his prosperity. During his early troubles, while supported by his only son Harith, he had felt so strongly his weakness and inferiority in contending with large and influential families of his opponents, that he vowed that if Allah should ever grant him ten sons, he would devote one of them to the Deity. Years rolled on, and the vow was granted. He bade his sons accompany him to Ka'abah ; each was made to write his name upon a lot, and the lots were made over to the Attendant of the Baitullah, who cast them in the usual manner.

The fatal arrow fell upon Abdullah, the youngest and the best beloved of Abd-ul Muttalib's sons. The vow must be kept, but how else should it be kept than by the sacrificial knife ?

His daughters wept and clung around the fond father, who was willingly persuaded to cast lots between Abdullah and ten camels, the current fine for the blood of a man, But the *lot* a second time fell upon Abdullah. Again, and with equal fortune, it was cast between him and twenty camels. At each successive trial Abdul Muttalib added ten camels to the stake, but the Deity appeared inexorably to re-fuse the offering and to require the blood of his son.

It was now tenth throw, and the ransom had reached a hundred camels, when the lot at last fell upon them. The father joyfully released Abdullah from his impending fate, and taking a hundred camels slaughtered them between Safa and Marwah. The inhabitants of Makkah feasted upon them ; and the residue was left to the beasts and the birds ; for Abdul Muttalibs' family refused to taste of them.

Abdul Muttalib had six daughters and it was one of them who made the proposal to cast lots for the camel.[1]

Waqidi says the Quraish held back Abdul Muttalib just as he was about to plunge the knife into his son, and offered to give a ransom, but he would not listen, at last they persuaded him to refer the matter to a divineress at Khaiber who indicated the plan of ransom described in the text above.

The people of Makkah had implicit faith In the Diplomatic tact and wisdom of Abdul Muttalib. Yemen at that time was ruled by Abraha, a bigoted Christian. He is described to us by the historians as a short, fat man who harboured a burning desire to destroy the Ka'abah and divert its pilgrims to Sana in Yemen, transfer all the wealth of the sanctuary to where he had built a magnificent Cathederal as a rival Sanctuary to

1. This account is from Kitab al-Waqidi p. 16 See also a paper in the Zeitschrift der Deutschen Morgenlandischen Gesellschaft, vii.i, p. 340.

Ka'abah. In future, he calculated, the pilgrims would bring their donations and offerings to his cathedral.

Abraha first launched a vigorous propaganda extolling the sanctity of his own church and defaming the Ka'abah. To Negus, the King of Ethiopia, Abraha wrote, "I have built a church for you, 0 King, such as has not been built for any king before you. I shall not rest until I have diverted the Arab's pilgrimage to it".[1]

Abraha waited for a pretext to attack Makkah, plunder its wealth and destroy the Ka'abah. To men of aggressive designs, the opportunity offers itself easily enough. It so happened that a party of Makkan merchants was staying in Sana. One of them had the temerity to defile the Cathederal. When he heard of it, Abraha was beside himself with rage and almost at once set out to conquer Hijaz.

Arriving at a point some distance from the city Abraha sent Hunata the Hamyarite to Makkah instructing him to enquire who was the Chief notable of the country and to tell him that the Kintg's message was that he had not come to fight them, but only to destroy the Ka'abah. If they did not resist him, he would not fight them; therefore, if the Makkans wished to avoid war, their chief should come and wait upon the King Abraha well knew that Abdul Muttalib was the leading

1. Ibn-i-Ishaque, *Sirat Rasul Allah,* op. cit. p. 22.

chief of Hejaz and to make sure that he would come as a suppliant to him, Abraha had seized two hundred camels belonging to Abdul Muttalib. When Hunata delivered Abiaha's message to the Makkans, they unanimously appointed Abdul Muttalib to act as their Stateman and Military Commander at this hour of peril. Abdul Muttalib said to Hunata : "Allah knows that we do not wish to light him (Abraha), for we have not the power to do so. This is Allah's sanctuary and the place of worship of His friend Abraham. If He defends it against him it is His Sanctuary ; and if He lets him have it, by Allah we cannot defend it !"

Hunata replied that he must come with him to Abraha, for he was ordered to bring him back with him. So accompanied by one of his sons Abdul Muttalib came to the Camp and enquired for Dhu Nafr, for he was a friend of his. Sometime previously Abraha had passed a death sentence upon Dhu Nafr and he was under confinement. Abdul Muttalib went to see him in his prison cell. Dhu Nafr said to Abdul Muttalib, "what use is a man held a prisoner is the hands of a King, expecting to be killed at any moment ? I can do nothing to help you except that Unays the keeper of the Elephant being a friend of mine I will send to him and commend your case to him as strongly as possible. So ' speak as you think fit and he will intercede for you with the King if he is able to do so".

Dhu Nafr sent to Unays, saying :

"The King has taken two hundred camels belonging to 'Abdul Muttalib, Lord of Quraish and Master of the Makkah well who feeds men in the plain and wild creatures on the top of the maintains and is now here. So help him as far as you can".

Now Abdul Muttalib was a most impressive, handsome and dignified man, and when Abraha saw him he treated him with the greatest respect so that he would not let him sit beneath him.

So he got off his throne and sat upon his carpet and made Abdul Muttalib sit beside him there. Then he told his interpreter to inquire what he wanted. Abdul Muttalib asked the King to return two hundred camels of his which he had taken. Abraha replied through the interpreter "you pleased as much when I saw you ; But I was much displeased with you when heard what you said. Do you wish to talk to me about two hundred camels of yours which I have taken, and say nothing about your religion and the religion of your forefathers which I have come to destroy ?"

Abdul Muttalib replied, "I am the owner of the camels and the temple has an owner who will defend it". When the King replied that he could not defend it against him, he said "That remains to be seen". Some learned people allege that when Abdul Muttalib went to Abraha when he sent Hunata to him, there accompanied him Yamur, bin Nufatha bin Adiy bin al-Du'il bin Bakr bin Abd Manat bin Kinana, at that time Chief of bin Bakr and Khuwaylid bin Wathila, then Chief of Hudayl. They offered to give Abraha a third of the cattle of low land on condition that he would withdraw from them and not destroy the ternple, but he refused their request, but Allah knows whether this was so or not. At any rate Abraha restored to Abdul Muttalib the camels which he had taken.

When they left him, Abdul Muttalib went back to Quraish and having given them the news ordered them to withdraw from Makkah and take up defensive positions on the peaks and in the passes of the mountains for fear of the excesses of the soldiers. He actually directed their military movements on this occasion apart from acting as an ambassador.

Abdul Muttalib took hold of the metal knocker of the Ka'abah, and a number of Quraysh stood with him praying to Allah and imploring his help against Abraha and his army. As he was holding the knocker of the temple door, Abdul Muttalib said :

"O Allah ! a man protects his dwelling. So protect thy dwellings. Let not their cross and their craft tomorrow overcome thy craft."

Al-Waqidi reports that Abdul Muttalib also said, "If you, Allah, are going to abandon them and our place of prayer, then something. Seemeth best to thee.

Abdul Muttalib then let go the knocker of the door of Ka'abah and went off with his Quraish companions to the mountain tops where they took up defensive positions waiting to see what Abraha would do when he occupied Makkah. In the morning Abraha prepared to enter the town and made his elephant ready for battle and drew up his troops. His intention was to destroy the Ka'abah and then return to Yemen.

Then Allah sent upon them birds from the sea like swallows and starlings ; each bird carried three stones of the size of peas and lentils, one in his beak and two between its claws. Everyone who was hit, died ; but not everyone was hit. They withdrew in flight by the way they came, crying out for Nufayl bin Habib to guide them on the way to Yemen.

As they withdrew they were continually falling by the wayside dying miserably by every water hole. Abraha was smitten in his body and as they took him away his fingers fell off one by one. Where the finger had been there arose an evil sore exuding pus and blood.

Yaqub bin Utba told me that he was informed that that year was the first time that measles and small-pox had been seen in Arabia.[1]

The defeat of Abraha is mentioned in the Qur'an. "Did you not see how your Lord dealt with the owners of the Elephant? Did he not reduce their guile to sheer terror ? And sent upon them flocks of birds, throwing hard clay stones upon them, making them as blades of corn that have been devoured." (Fiel : 1-5)

This later simile is a good description of the ravages of small-pox on human body.

Regarding Abdul Muttalib's local and international prestige, William Muir writes:

The foreign relations of Coreish were managed solely by the sons of Abd Menaf. With the Roman authorities and the Ghassanide Prince, Hashim himself concluded a treaty. He received from the Emperor a rescript authorising the Coreish to travel to and from Syria in security. It is added that as often as he went to Ankhra (Ancyra) he was admitted to the presence of the Emperor, who honoured and esteemed him.[2]

The former says that both the Ceasar and Nejashy honoured and loved him.

1. Ibn-i-Ishaque pp. 22-26.
2. See also *Kitab aA-Waqidi,* p. 13-13 ; Tabari, p. 23 (Muir, *ibid* pp. CCXLIV).

Hashim also secured the friendship of the inhabitants on the road, by promising to carry their goods without hire. Hia brother Abd Shams made a treaty with Najashy in pursuance of which the Coreish traded to Abyssinia ; his other brothers, Naufal and Al-Muttalib concluded alliances, the former with the King of Persia who allowed them to traffic in Iraq and Fars, the latter with the Kings of Himyar, who encouraged their commercial operation in Yemen. Thus the affairs of the Coreish prospered in every direction.

To Hashim is ascribed the credit of establishing upon a uniform footing the mercantile expeditions of his people, so that every winter a caravan sent out regularly for Yemen and Abyssinia, while in the summer a second visited Ghazza, Ancyra and the other Syrian marts.

Abdul Muttalib was generous, large-hearted gallant, bold, high-minded, hospitable, gracious and an eminent just man. Acknowledging these virtues the Quraish had appointed him their Sardar (Leader). The life and character of Abdul Muttalib is well depicted by the Elegies composed on his death by his daughters. Ibn-i-Ishaque reports :

"Mohammad bin Said bin al-Mussayib told me that when Abdul Muttalib knew that death was at hand he summoned his six daughters, Safiya, Barra, Atika,

Umm Hakim al-Bayda, Umayma and Arwa and said to them, 'Compose Elegies over me so that I may hear what you are going to way before I die."

Safiya said in mourning her father :

"I could not sleep for the voices of the weening woman,
Bewailing a man on the crown of life's road.
It caused the tears to flow.
Down my cheeks like falling pearls.
For a noble man, no wretched weakling,
Whose virtue was plan to all.
The generous Shayba, full of merits,
Thy good father inheritor of all virtue
Truthful at home, no weakling,
Standing firm and self-reliant.
Powerful, fear-inspiring, massive,
Praised and obeyed by his people,
Of lofty lineage, smiling, virtuous
A very rain when camels had no milk.[1]

---

1. Tradition relates that Abdul Muttalib's body emitted a fragrance like musk-scent and he had a refulgence in the forehead. To obtain respite from the season of

[Cont.]

Noble was his grandfather without spot of shame,

Surpassing all men, bond or free,

Exceeding mild, of noble stock,

Who were generous, strong as lions,

Could men be immortal through ancient glory,

(Alas, immortality is unobtainable)

He would make his last night endure for ever.
Through his surpassing glory and long descent.[1]

His daughter Barra said :

Be generous, O eyes, with your pearly tears,

For the generous nature who never repelled a beggar.

Of glorious race, successful in under-taking,

Of handsome face, of great nobility.

Shayba, the laudable, the noble,

The glorious, the mighty, the renowned,

The clement, decisive in misfortunes,

---

draught the Quraish used to perform a ritual. Holding his hand they took Ahdul Muttalib to the mountain of Shabbir and asked him to pray there for rainfall. Abdul Muttalib's prayer was often answered and the dry spell came to an end.

1. Saffia's dirge depicts a brave, truthful, smiling, mild, yet an awe-inspiring man of massive presence.

Full of generosity lavish in gifts,
Excelling his people in glory,
A light shining like the moon in its splendour.
Death came to him and spared him not.
Change and fortune and fate overtook him.[1]
His daughter Atika said :
Be generous, O eyes, and not niggardly
With your tears when other sleep,
Weep copiously, O eyes, with your tears,
While you beat your faces in weeping.
Weep, O eyes, long and freely.
For one, no dotard weakling,
The strong, generous in time of need,
Noble in purpose, faithful to his word.
Shayba the laudable, successful in undertaking,
The reliable and the steady,
A sharp sword in war
Destroying his enemies in battle,
Easy-natured, open-handed,
Loyal, stout, pure, good.

1. Barra celebrates the generous qualities of Abdul Muttalib.

His house proudly rooted in high honour
Mounted to glory unobtainable by others.[1]
His daughter Umm Hakim al-Bayda said :
Weep, O eye, generously, hide not thy tears,
Weep for the liberal and generous one,
Fie upon thee O eye, help me.
With fast falling tears !
Weep for the best man who ever rode a beast,
Thy good father, a fountain of sweet water.
Shayba the generous, the virtuous,
Liberal in nature, praised for his gifts
Lavish to his family, handsome,
Welcome as rain in years of drought.
A lion when the spears engage,
His womenfolk look on him proudly.
Chief of Kinana on whom their hopes
When evil days brought calamity,
Their refuge when war brok out,
In trouble and dire distress.
Weep for him, refrain not from grief.

---

1. Atika describes her father as a chivalrous chief.

Make women weep for him as long as you live.[1]

His daughter Umaima said :

Alas has the shepherd of his people,
Tho generous one, perished,
Who gave the pilgrims their water,
Tho defender of our fame.
Who used to gather the wandering guest into his tents,
When the heavens begrudged their rain.
You have the noblest sons a man could have.
And have never ceased to grow in fame, O Shayba !
Abu'l Harith, the bountiful, has left his place,
Go not far for every living thing must go far.
I shall weep for him and suffer as long as I live.
His memory deserves that I suffer.
May the Lord of men water thy grave with rain.
I shall weep for him though he lies in the grave.
He was the pride of all his people,
And was praised whereever praise was due.[2]

---

1. In Umm Hakim Al-Bayda's eyes he was the epitome of ideal manhood. He was gallant in war, generous in peace, a philanthropist and a selfless leader of men.
2. Umaima Celebrates the charitable actes and Hospitality of Abdul Muttalib.

His daughter Arwah said :

My Eye wept and well it did for the generous modest father

The pleasant natured man of Makkah's' Vale.

Noble in mind, lofty in aim,

The bountful Shayba, full of virtues.

Thy good father who has no pear,

Long-armed, Elegant, tall.

'Twas as though his forehead shone

Lean-waisted, handsome, full of virtues,

Glory, rank and dignity were his,

Resenting wrong, Smiling, able,

His ancestral fame could not be hid,

The refuge of Malik,,

The Spring of Fihr,

When judgement was sought he spoke the last word.

He was a hero, generous, liberal.

When armed men were afraid of death so that the hearts of most of them were air,[1]

---

1. See Surah (Ibrahim : 44) of the Quran "and their heart were air."

Forward he went with gleaming Sword;

The Cynosure of all Eyes.

Mother and sisters wiere deemed most worthy to mourn and praise him.

A Western Literary Historian notes that "the high-born women of Arabia had gracious dignity and quick intelligence and passionate affection. Many among them had the gift of poetry, which they bestowed especially on the dead. The hero's mother and sisters were deemed most worthy to mourn and praise him".[1]

In regard to the tradition of writing elegiac poetry the same author says :

The poetry of Arabian women of the Pre-Islamic period is distinctly masculine in character. Their songs are seldom of Love, but often of Death. Elegy (ritha or marthiya) was regarded as their special province. As a rule, the Arabian dirge is very simple. The poetess begins with a description of her grief, of the tears that she cannot quench, and then she shows how worthy to be deeply mourned was he whom death has taken away. He is described as the pattern of the two principal virtues, bravery and liberality, and the question is anxiously asked.

1. Reynolds A. Nicholson, A Literary History of Arabia [Cambridge, 1953], p. 87.

"Who will now make high resolves, overthrow the Enemy, and in time of want feed the poor and entertain the stranger? " It is impossible to translate the vivid Emotion, the Energy of Passion and noble simplicity of style which distinguish these Elegies"?[1] Historical Evidence suggests that nearly all the forebears of Abdullah occupied preeminent positions in their times.

Among the illustrious ancestors of the family were three prophets, Ibrahim, Ismael and Idrees (who, it is said, invented the art of writing) (Peace be upon all of them).

It was, therefore, a family so high in the favour of Allah that He had specially reserved it for Electing His earthly Messengers from it.

Traditions of the Holy Prophet (peace be upon him) and utterances of the venerable companions (Allah be pleased with them) all suggest that the ancestors of the Holy Prophet (peace be upon him) professed the religion of the Prophet Ibrahim, that is, they were Hanif,[2] worshippers of One and only Allah. Anas reports ; The Holy Prophet (peace be upon him) racited this verse لقد جاء كم رسول من انفسكم which means:

---

1. *Ibid.*, p. 87.
2. See the last chapter where the term has been exhaustively discussed in the light of the verses of the Quran.

"No doubt there came to you the Messengers of Allah, your superiors, better than you and rising for noblest families".

After reciting this verse the Holy Prophet (peace be upon him) observed : "In respect of ancestry, I am better than all of you. Among my ancestors from Adam to the present generation no one has committed adultery. They all contracted proper marriages".

'(Rawah ibn Marduya, *Zarqani Sharah Muwahab,* p. 67).

When Emperor Heracles of Rome questioned Abu Sufian about the Holy Prophet and asked :

"Say, what his ancestry is like ?" It is recorded in Sahih Bukhari that Abu Sufian replied : "He has the noblest ancestry of us all". Hafiz Asqiani says that the tradition related by Bazzar has the following words :

"No one excels him in Exalted ancestry and nobility of family".[1]

Hearing this the Emperor Heracles observed : "Yes, this is one of the attributes of Prophets". Some traditions as recorded by Bukhari say that upon hearing

---

1. *Fateh-al-Bari,* vol. 8, Kitab al-Tafsir.

the answer of Abu Sufain, the Roman Emperor remarked :

"The Prophets always spring from noble families."[2]

2. Idrees Kandhalvi, *Sirat-e-Mustafa* (Jamia Ashrafia, Lahore), p, 10.

ABDULLAH'S BIRTH AND CHILDHOOD

Abdul Muttalib had seven high-born, beautiful and virtuous wives. Their names were :

1. Mona bint Harith Kalab.
2. Sumaira binat Ghadiq Taliq.
3. Hajara Khaza.
4. Saada bint Habib Kalab.
5. Hala bint Wahab.
6. Fatima bint Umar Mahzoomi.
7. Fatima Nateela.

Fatima bint Umar Mahzami[1] was the mother of Abdullah. Tradition relates that a short time before Fatima became pregnant with Abdullah, Abdul Muttalib had gone to the forest to hunt.

After a day's chase he was overcome by fatigue and thirst. Suddenly he came upon a spring whose water was colder than snow and sweeter than honey. Abdul Muttalib drank the water and the thought came to him

1. Fatima binat Umar Mahzoomi was thus the paternal grandmother of Prophet Muhammad (peace be on him).

what other place except Paradise can hold such cold and sweet water.

Abdul Muttalib sired twelve sons and six daughters whose names are as follows :[1]

1. Harith, the eldest son was born in 528 A.D. (Harith had five sons : Mughira, Abu Sufian, Naufal, Abdullah and Rabea).
2. Abdul Azza or Abu Lahab (who was the cruellest tormentor of Muhammad (peace be upon him) was born in 540 A.D. (Abu Lahab had two sons Utaiba and Atiba. Utaiba's wife was the aunt of Amir Muwayia).
3. Abd Manaf popularly known as Abu Talib. (he had four sons Uqqil, Talib, Jaafer Tayer, and Ali; and two daughters, Amhani and Rahmani) Abu Talib's date of birth is 540 A.D.

4 & 5. Zubair and Abdullah were born of Fatima bint Umar Mahzoomi in 545 A.D. Fatima also gave birth to Atiqa, Umama, Urwa, Bara and Um-al-Hakam alias al-Baiza.[2]

6&7. Between 556-622 A.D. Zarar and Abbas were born of Nateela. (Abbas had six sons : Abdullah,

1. Amir Ali, *Prophet of Islam*, p. 19.
2. Zubair, therefore was the full uncle of the Holy Prophet and Atiqa, Umaima, Urwa, Bara and Um-al-Hakam were his full aunts. Syed Amir Ali says that Abdullah was born in 24th year of the Coronation of Nusherwan the Just, King of Persia.

Fazal, Ubaid-ullah, Qusum, Saeed, Abdur Rehman and one daughter, Saffia).

8, 9, 10. Maqum and Jehm (whose title was Al-Ghaidak) and Hamza (who was one of the first to embrace Islam). Ghaidaq, Zarar, and Zubair were issueless.

11,12,13. Qusum, Abdul Kaaba and Jamal born of Hala bint Wahab. Hala was also the mother of a girl Saffiya. (Saffiya was the grandmother of the famous historical personage Abdullah ibn-i-Zubair).

As mentioned above Abdullah was born of Fatima bint Umar Mahzoomi in 545 A.D.

Abdullah's childhood was Spent in a large and prosperous family and he probably enjoyed every comfort that money could buy, for Abdul Muttalib, his father, was a man of considerable means. All evidence suggests that Abdul Muttalib had provided the finest education and training for his sons and daughters. The intellectual capacity of Abdullah's sisters may be estimated from the above quoted Elegies, which bear witness to the fact that the family had a well-developed literary taste and all its members were intelligent and urbane.

Prosperity and cohesion must have generated an atmosphere of family bliss. Abdullah was the pet of his father, and a favourite of his brothers and sisters. Harith, the eldest brother, especially loved him. All the sisters adored him for his good looks and gentle manners. Abdullahs' maternal uncles and aunts too were deeply attached to him. Evidently, therefore, he must have been a happy child. His education must have followed the pattern which was current among contemporary commercial families. He must have learnt the folk tales, folk ballads, poetry and oral history of Arabia and possibly tales brought to Makkah by merchants from foreign lands, from China, Persia and the Roman Empire. He must have learnt arithmetic, accounting, reading and writing which were indispensable qualifications for the commercial career which he later adopted.

As for his religious training we can safely assert that he was imbued with the same religious beliefs which his illustrious family had held since the time of Prophet Ibrahim (peace be on him).

The followers of Ibrahim have been referred to in the Quran as Hanif, or Hunafa, the worshippers of one Allah.

A note on 'Hanif' in the *Shorter Encyclopaedia of Islam*[1] says :

1. Leiden.

"Hanif" appears repeatedly in the Quran as the name of those who possess the real and true religion, *e.g.* in surah x: 105 ; xxii: 31 ; xxx: 30 ; xcviii: 4 etc.

It is used particularly of Abraham as the representative of the pure worship of Allah. As a rule it contrasts him with the idolaters as in iii: 95 ; vi: 79, 161; x: 104 ; xvi: 120, 123 ; xxii: 31. But in one or two passages the same time describes him as one who was neither a jew nor a Christian ; *e.g.* ii: 135. "They (the Ahl-e-Kitab) say," become Jews or Christians that ye may be rightly guided. But thou shalt say : the religion of Abraham as a hanif ; he was not one of the Polytheists" ; and iii: 67 ; "Abraham was neither Jew nor Christian, but Hanif Muslim and was not one of the Polytheists."

Sura xxx: 30 is of special importance for the understanding of the Quranic meaning of the word, where it is said, "Turn thy face towards religion as hanif, (namely) Allah's Creation *(fitra)* according to which he has created man, there is no change in the work of Allah" ; *of* also vi: 79 ; x: 105. It is clear here that the word means the original, innate, primitive religion in contrast to the particular religions which arose later, Polytheism on the one hand and in part corrupt religions of the possessors of scriptures.

The Hanifiya means the religion of Abraham, *e.g.* Ibn Hisham, pp. 143, 147, 822. But as Muhammad renovated the pure religion of Abraham, hanif is frequently used in the sense of Muslim (Mohammadan), *e.g.* Ibn Hisham pp. 982, 995 ff also p. 871.

In various traditions the Prophet describes the religion proclaimed by him as al-Hanaifiya al-Samha the mild or liberal Hanifism in opposition to ascetic movements, *e.g.* Ibn Sad, 1/1/iii/i- 128, 287."

YOUTH AND MARRIAGE

Abdullah was uncommonly handsome. A hereditary quality of physical grace had been uniform among the descendants of Hashim. A man of strong physique and resplendent face he was commonly known in Makkah by the epithet "Lamp of the City."[1]

The news that Habal had demanded no less than a hundred camels as ransom for his life had greatly raised the reputation of Abdullah among the women.[2]

The fame of his manly beauty had spread far and wide. The women of Makkah, among them several high-born and cultured Christian and Jewish ladies adored Abdullah and longed for an intimate connection with him.

Their passion for Abdullah does not appear to have been wholly carnal. The Christian and Jewish scholars had long predicted the advent of a new Prophet and quite naturally anticipated the birth of this Prophet to occur in the clan descended from Prophets Abraham and Isaac (peace be on them).

1. Hyat ul-Kuloob p. 3.
2. Sirat-i-Rasul Mohd Husain Haikal Chapter I.

Tradition asserts that the light of Prophecy that shone in the forehead of Abraham (peace be on him) had been lineally transmitted to the male members of his progeny and the same light blazed with great intensity in the forehead of Abdullah. Abdullah's Christian and Jewish admirers had therefore a spiritual motive also.

They coveted the honour of bearing a Prophet. Qatila bint Naufal and Fatimar bint Mur have been most frequently mentioned by the historians as most ardent pursuers of Abdullah.

Qatila was the sister of Warraqqa bin Naufal.[1] Traditions about her state :

After the incident of casting lots for Abdullah "taking Abduallah by the hand Abdul Muttalib went

---

1. Warakka's name frequently finds honourable mention in the early history of Muhammad (peace be on him). Waraqqa waa the first to testify that Muhammad was the Prophet whose advent earlier Divine Books had promised. A note in the *shoter Encyclopaedia of Islam* says :

   It was Waraqqa who found the infant Muhammad when he straved from his nurse. Khadija, whose cousin he was consulted him on her marriage, of which Waraqqa warmly approved. One of the earliest confidants of the first revelation, he told Muhammad that Jesus had predicted his mission that he had been visit-ed by the Namus who came to Moses and foretold his career and final triumph. It was also Waraqqa who

[Cont. to 38]

away and they passed —so it is alleged—a woman of bint Asad bin Abdul-Uzza bin Qusavy bin Kitab bin Murra bin Kab bin Luayy bin Ghalib bin Fihr who was the sister of Waraqqa bin Naufal bin Asad bin Abdul Uzza, who was at the Kaaba. When she looked at him she asked, "where are you going Abdullah?" He replied "with my father." She said, "if you will take me you can have as many camels as were sacrificed in your stead."

"I am with my father and I cannot act against his wishes and leave him," he replied."[1]

---

consoled Bilal when tormented by his pagan master.

Ibn Hisham p. 100-101, 107, 143, 149, 153-154, 205; al-Tabari, i: 1147-1152. Ibn Said, 1/i:58, 130, Ibn al Athir Usd al-Ghaba v: 88 ; Ibn Hadfar, Isaba Cairo 1325, vi: 317 ; Kitab al-Aghani iii: 14-15.

Ibn Hisham writes :

That Warqqa had rejected idolatry and left his home in order to seek the true religion of Abraham. Waraqqa became a Christian. He abstained from idol-worship, from eating that what had died of itself, from blood, and from the flesh of animals offered in sacrifice to idols ; he condemned the barbarous custom of burying female infants alive, and said, "I worship the Lord of Abraham."

1. Ibn Ishaque, *Sirat Rasul-Allah,* trans. A. Guillaum (Oxford University Press, 1955) p. 68.

In *Tabqat,* Ibn-e-Saad narrates the same tradition in this manner.

"Once Qatila bint Naufal, who was young at that time, came before Abdullah ibn Muttalib and laying her hand on him offered herself in marriage to him. Abdullah ibn Muttalib repulsed her and quickly quitted her presence. Meanwhile Abdullah married Amina (or Amna) and she conceived the Apostle.

Later, on seeing Qatila again Abdullah ibn Muttalib remarked to her "Do you wish to marry me now?" She said' "No ! when I saw you the previous time I observed a light in your forehead and I wanted to get it. This light I no longer see in your forehead. She whose share it was, has taken it."[1]

Tibri records a similar episode about Fatima bint Mur, the beautiful and cultured daughter of a wealthy Jew.

"Ibn Abbas reported that when Abdul Muttalib was taking his son Abdullah to arrange his marriage, they passed by a learned Jewess belonging to the tribe of Bani Khatham. Her name was Fatima bint Mur and she was wellread in the scriptures of the Jews. She observed a remarkable radiance in the forehead of

1. Ibn Sa'ad, *Tabqati-See* also Aulad Haider Bilgrami, *Sirat-e-Rasul* (Agra).

Abdullah and said to him "O Swain, if you consent to perform intercourse with me here and now I shall present you a hundred camels".

Abdullah replied :

اما الحرام فالمات دونه، والحل لا حل فاستبيله فكيف

بالامر الذى تبغينه

"Impossible. Death before illicit intercourse. This is not lawful. How can then that come to pass which you desire"?[1] Another report of the above incident is as follows :

"Ibn Abbas says, when Abdul Muttalib was taking Abdullah to arrange his marriage, they passed by a Jewess by name Fatima Bint Mur. She was well-versed in Torah and Injil (Bible). She observed a refulgence in the forehead of Abdullah and calling him to her side, said, "I will present you with one hundred camels." Abdullah recited these verses in reply :

اما الحرام فالمات دونه والحل لا حل فاستبينه

"Death is better than sin and I will not do that which I cannot admit with clear conscience."

فكيف با الامر الذى تبغينه، يحمى الكريم عرصه و دينه.

1. Tibri, i.

"How can I meet with your unholy desire. A pure man guards his honour and faith with full strength." When Abdullah returned after his marriage with Amina, he chanced to meet Fatima again. She said, "O Abdullah, where have you been since I last saw you ?" Abdullah replied, "I married Amna the daughter of Wahb bin Abd Munaf and stayed with my in-laws for three days."

On hearing this the Jewess answered, "By Allah, I am no loose woman. Noticing the light of prophecy in your forehead, I wished to receive it in my womb. But Allah has transferred it to where it pleased Him."[1]

These traditions leave no doubt that though the women generally in that period of ignorance were inclined to immorality, but Atiqa bint Naufal and Fatima Binat Mur were not entirely moved by carnal desire. They were not only attracted to the physical but also the spiritual beauty of Abdullah.

On the other hand, at a time and place where adulterous connections with beautiful and accomplished women were considered the very mark of manhood, Abdullah's constant refusal to commit adultery reveals a strong and faithful personality.

---

1. Mohammad Idrees Kandhalvi, *Sirat Mustafa'*, (Lahore), p. 34.

"Adultery, homicide, drinking, stealing and damaging and devouring other people's property was common. These vices were so rampant in the pre-Islamic Arabian Society that people had become used to them. These vices had become "folk crimes".. Adultery meaning all those acts of sexual relationship which do not fall in the area of marriage was never favoured by the pre-Islamic Arabs, but it was certainly a matter of pride especially for the male who engaged in it. Men would eye at other people's wives. Or, they would have relations with women over a prolonged period of time without any marital obligations.

This high sexual mobility on the part of the male was the subject of prideful boasts especially in the male company.[1] This intense regard for moral purity was certainly developed in Abdullah by disciplined training at home. There is no doubt whatsoever that in this family of Prophets there had existed an unbroken tradition of moral rectitude since the times of Ibrahim (Abraham), Yakub, (Jacob) and Ishaque (Isaac). Muhammad (peace be upon him) justly landed the purity of his ancestors. Anas reported, "The Holy Prophet (Peace be upon him) rented this verse of the Quran :

---

1. Ilyas Ba Yunus 'Crime in the Pre-Islamic Arabia', *Journal Rabetat Al-Alarm. Al-Islami,* Makkah, Feb/March 1978, pp : 72-73).

"No doubt Allah sent among you His Apostles and raised them from the most exalted and noblest families among you".

Having recited the verse, the Holy Prophet (peace be upon him) observed. In respect of genealogy I am the best among you. Of my ancestors since Adam none has committed adultery. All made marriages".[1]

Wahab and Waheeb, two brothers, of the tribe of Bani Zohra, lived in the suburbs of Makkah. They were merchants of respectable means. Wahab's daughter Amina (the other popular rendering of her name is "Amna" was endowed with beauty and grace and excelled in virtue. She was under the charge of her uncle Waheeb. The following traditions relate the story of her marriage with Abdullah :

"When Abdul Muttalib heard that his son Abdullah was the object of several women's affections and proposals of marriage came pouring in from all sides, he paid a visit to the house of Amina's uncle Waheeb. The latter happily agreed to give his niece's hand in marriage to Abdullah. So Abdullah married Amina and on the same auspicious day Abdul Muttalib married Waheeb's daughter Hala, who bore Hamza, later the champion of Islam. Hala was wet nurse to infant

1. Hafiz Idrees Kandhalvi, *Sirat Mustafa,* Vol I, Maktaba Usmania, Lahore p. 10.

Muhammad (peace be on him) and so Hamza, was both an uncle and foster brother of the Prophet".[1] In another tradition the marriage ceremony is described in such a way that it reminds one of the Islamic form of marriage. According to arrangement, Abdul Muttalib, with his illustrious cousins in elegant attire, met Wahab and his relatives and when all were assembled, Abdul Muttalib introduced the business by rising and chanting an ode of the greatest elegance and beauty, saying I praise Allah with thanks giving and praises which He inspires by the favours which He has bestowed upon us. He has made us the neighbours of His own House, (a reference to Ka'abah in Makkah, founded by Ibrahim (Abraham) as a House of the worship of one Allah. Later converted into a temple housing many gods (made of stone and wood), inhabitants of the sacred city and inspired love for us in the hearts of His servants. He has exalted us over other sects and protected us from calamity and misfortune. I render thanks to the Lord Who has made marriage lawful to us and forbidden illicit intercourse.

Now, be it known, that our son Abdullah solicits in marriage your daughter Amina, and offers such a marriage settlement do you accept his proposal, or do

---

1. Hameedullah Beg Dehlvi, *Rauof-ul-Rahim* Karachi (1961) Chapter I, also *Tareekh Al-Khamees Ajaib-ul-Hakayat.*

you not ? Wahab replied, we accept ; to which Abdul Muttalib rejoined, By ye all witnesses of the solemn engagement. He then gave in behalf of his son a nuptial feast which lasted four days to which all the people of Makkah and its territories were invited".[1]

Ibn Hisham, Ibn Sa'ad, Tibri, Ibn Kathir and Abul-Fida, almost all Arab historians have dated the event of Abdullah's marriage after the episode of the people of the Elephant (Abraha's advance on Makkah) and yet these same historians put the date of Abraha's attack only fifty days before the birth of Muhammad (peace be upon him). The fact ia that Arab authors are more concerned with the recording of events and less with their sequence. Hence they show now particular regard for the precise dating of incidents.

The historians also differ in regard to the age of Abdullah at the time of his marriage with Amina. Ibn Sa'ad states that Abdullah was 17 years old when he married Amina. Ibn Sa'ad also reports that the proposal of marriage had been initiated not by Abdul Muttalib but by the family of Amina.

Bani Zuhra dwelt in the suburbs of Makkah. Abdul Muttalib rejected the proposals that came on

1. *Hyat-ul-Kaloob* translated from Persian under the title "The Life and Religion of Muhammad" by James L-Merick (Boston 1850) pp. 29-31).

behalf of the daughters of the chiefs and notables of Makkah and neighbouring lands and readily accepted the proposal that came from the Bani Zuhra. He married his son Abdullah to Amna bint Wahab and himself married Hala bint Waheeb on the same day. Waheeb was younger than Wahab and, therefore, next in line for the chiefship of his tribe. These two sons of Abdul Munaf ibne Zuhra ibne Kalab were men of power and authority in their tribe. Amna was the ward of her uncle Waheeb and it was to Waheeb's house that Abdul Muttalib took his son Abdullah and solemised his marriage with Amna. Abdul Muttalib himself married Hala, the daughter of Waheeb, at the same time"[1]

Kalab, the ancestor of Wahab and Waheeb, was also the forebear of Abdul Muttalib. Between the family of Hashim and the Bani Zuhra, there existed a long-standing relationship. This explains why out of numerous proposals submitted to him for the hand of his son from many quarters the request that came from Bani Zuhra was more acceptable to Abdul Muttalib. The proposal from Bani Zuhra is reported to have originated, because Wahab on one occasion was deeply impressed by the extraordinary bravery of Abdullah.

The tradition is *Hyat-ul-Kuloob* re-lates : "The Yehoodee priests of Sham (Jewish Rabbis of Syria),

1. Ibn-i-Sa'ad, *Tabqat,* Vol I P. 58.

being apprised of the extraordinary characteristics which distinguished Abdullah began to talk of the last Prophet, which by their books, they concluded to be near. After consulting with a celebrated wise man of theirs, who, however discouraged their enterprise, a plot was formed for cutting off Abdullah and thus preventing the ruin of their own faith by the religion soon to be promulgated. A party with poisoned sword were despatched to Makkah for the ostensible purpose of trade, who were to watch an opportunity for assassinating the young and distinguished Chief. On arriving at Makkah they demanded such an extravagant price for their goods that no one would purchase, and thus a pretext was furnished for their continuing in the city. During this time Abdullah dreamed that some apes attacked him sword in hand, but he was raised up in the air, and fire came down from heaven and cansumed them. On relating this dream to Abdul Muttalib, he said Allah will protect you my son, from all calamities, but you should be aware that many are envious of the light which distinguishes you, and may attempt your destruction. Abdullah generally hunted in company with his father who so overawed the murderous infidels that no attempt was made on the life of the young chief. At length he went alone on a huntting excursion, and the party from Sham, thinking it a very favourable opportunity for their purpose, stationed some of their number to take care of their goods, and concealing their sword under their garments, started in pursuit and overtook the young hero just as he was entering a narrow defile of the mountains and intent on despatching some game. They immediately inclosed him in the defile and Abdullah, perceiving their design to kill him raised his head and implored help from the Omniscient, and then turning to his assailants, demanded why they were attempting his life, as he had never injured one of them, or anyone belonging to them, in property or in person. Without stopping to answer, they rushed upon him, while he, pronouncing the sacred name of Allah, discharged four arrows, which sent as many of the party to perdition. The infidels, now recurring to stratagem, cried out "Why are you killing us at such a rate? We have no design on you. One of our slaves has run away, and seeing you at a distance, we thought you were the man". Abdullah laughing at this barefaced lie, mounted his horse, and bow in hand, attempted to quit their company upon which they renewed the attack with stones and swords, but he charged upon them like a lion and dashed a number of them to destruction.

Being closely beset, he dismounted, and putting his back to a cliff, was worried by the stones hurled at him, his assailants not venturing to come hand to hand.

In these desperate circumstances, Wahab the son of Abdul Minaf happened to enter the defile, but not venturing to engage so many, he set off for the Ka'abah and shouted among the Bani Hasham, "Rescue Abdullah, enemies have beset him in such a ravine." Instantly the Bani Hashim seized their swords and vaulted upon their unsaddled horses, and flew to the defile. As soon as Abdul Muttalib and his party approached, he shouted to his son saying, this is the interpretation of your dream. At this unexpected attack the Yehoodees were in utter despair, some, however, fled to a fissure in the mountain where by divine power a rock rolled down and crushed them to death. A few of the party, who entreated that sufficient truce might be granted to allow them to settle their account at Makkah were spared immediate death, and having their hands tied were taken back to the city, where on their entrance, the people cast stones at them and cursed them. Abdul Muttalib sent them to be imprisoned in the house of Wahab who had given notice of their attack on Abdullah. Wahab, on returning home, said to his wife, O Berah, I have witnessed a number of things to-day respecting Abdullah which I never saw before in reference to any Arab hero. Allah has endowed him with beauty, elegance and light in a peculiar manner, so that his equal has never been seen or heard of. When the Yehoodees attacked him, I saw hosts of angels descend from heaven to give him the victory. Go now, my Berah, to Abdul Muttalib and petition him to accept our daughter Aminah, as a wife for Abdullah, and ennoble us by the Alliance. She replied, you know, my husband, that all the chiefs of Makkah, and kings of the surrounding regions, have aspired to such an alliance and been refused, how then will he incline to our daughter. Wahab rejoined, I have today imposed a great obligation on them by informing them of the danger which beset Abdullah. Possibly in consideration of that they may accept our daughter. When Berah entered the house of Abdul Muttalib he greeted her with a cordial welcome, adding, your husband has done us a great favour today and whatever you ask in return shall be granted. She replied, "My husband has sent me to make a great request of you, no less than to ask your acceptance of our daughter Aminah as a wife for Abdullah. We desire no dower, but present her as an offering to you". Abdul Muttalib looked at his illustrious son and said, "Although you have not accepted the daughter of kings, yet it is to be considered that this maiden is of your own kindred and there is no virgin in Makkah her equal in every accomplishment of mind and person. Abduallh modestly continued silent, but manifested no dislike to the proposed union, upon which his father said to Berah, your suit is granted.

In the evening Abdul Muttalib, accom-panied by his son, visited Wahab, and while they were all in conference together discussing the marriage, the captured Yehoodees succeeded in freeing themselves from the bonds, and arming themselves with stones furiously assaulted the deliberating chiefs, but through divine power and miraculous influence of the symbolic light of Prophecy, the stone hurled by each man recoiled on his head and breast, and instantly the fierce lions of heroism drew their swords and finished the business by sending all those infidels to perdition. Abdul Muttalib and Wahab then agreed to assemble their repective kindred early the next morning, and conclude the alliance so auspiciously begun.[1]

Allowing for the hyperbole and the introduction of the Supernatural in the above narration, one cannot really doubt the probability of the incident.[2]

After the nuptial ceremony Abdullah stayed in his bride's home for three days, as was the general custom in Arabia.[3]

Ibn Hisham writes, "Abdullah brought Amina to his paternal home and was intimated with her, as a result of which she conceived the illustrious Apostle".[4]

---

1. *Hyat-ul-Kuloob,* translated from Persian under the title "The Life and Religion of Muhammad" by Rev. James L. Merriok (Boston, 1850) pp. 30-31
2. The episode also furnishes evidence that the advent of a new Prophet was imminently expected and that the Jewish laity were considerably perturbed over this prospect.
3. Mohammad Hussain Haikal, *Sirat al-Rasul.*
4. Hisham, Vol. I.

From a tradition recorded by Ibn Ishaque it appears that Abdullah had another woman beside Amina.

Whether this woman was a wife or a slave girl, the tradition does not say. There is however strong reason to hold that this woman was another properly wedded wife of Abdullah. The evidence of Muhammad (peace be upon him) that in his family there had never been anything but proper marriages suffices to establish this point.

Recounting a domestic stroy Ibn-e-Ishaque writes:

> "My father Ishaque bin Yasar told *me* that he was told that Abdullah went in to a woman, that he had beside Amina bin Wahab when he had been working in clay and the marks of clay were on him. She put him off when he made a suggestion to her because of the dirt that was on him. He then left her and washed and bathed himself, and as he made his way to Amina he passed her and she invited him to come to her. He refused and went to Amina who conceived Muhammad. When he passed the woman again he asked her if she wanted anything and she said, "No ! when you passed me there was a white blaze between your eyes and when I invited you, you refused

me and went in to Amina, and she has taken it away."[1]

After he had consummated his marriage with Amna, Abdullah met Qatila bint Naufal again :

> "He asked her why she did not make the proposal that she made to him the day before ; to which she replied that the light that was with him the day before had left him, and she no longer had need of him. She had heard from her brother Waraqqa bin Naufal, who had been a Christian and studied the scriptures, that a prophet would arise among his people."[2]

According to a majority of traditions Amna had been pregnant with Muhammad (peace be upon him) for 8 eight months at the time of Abdullah's passing away. Abdullah had set out on his last trading journey about two months before his death. Thus he and Amna had lived together for six months only.

It can be fairly assumed that they must have passed this time in that wholesome ecstasy which is the privilege of a newly married couple. There is evidence that Amna already deeply adored her husband.[3]

---

1. (Ishaq's *Sirat Rasul* trans. A. Guillaum (Oxford 1955) p. 69.
2. *Ibid.*
3. See Amina's dirge on the death of Abdullah.

Certain it is also that Amna was the favourite of her in-laws. Out of many offers she had been especially selected as bride for his son by Abdul Muttalib himself. The family was welladjusted under the firm but benign control of Abdul Muttalib. Abdullah and his brothers and sisters were close to each other. As we have seen above, Abdul Muttalib's daughters had a fine sensibility and were amply endowed with literary talent. In such a cultured home, a young lady of beauty and refinement must have been warmly received and showered with affection and understanding. All traditions agree that Amna was wise, goodnatured and well-versed in household arts. It is only natural that she should have given entire satisfaction and earned the unbounded love of her husband.

ABDULLAH'S VOCATION

Describing the importance of Makkah as a commercial and trade centre in the 6th century B.C., a modern historian writes : "Makkah was a commercial city and a growing financial centre. It had originated as an entrepot but by the end of the 6th century Makkan merchants were buying and selling wares in all of the markets from Yemen to Damascus. The merchandise mainly consisted of camphor, dates and spices. Hadrmut, Yemen, Makkah, Hijaz and Damascus were in fact a chain of marts on the same international trade route which extended on the one end to India and China and on the other to Rome. There were several financial houses in Makkah owned or directed by a single person or by a company".[1]

These financial houses received and maintained deposits of money or gooda from the public and invested them in commercial ventures for profit or interest. There is little evidence of local industry in Makkah or the Hijaz. There were orchards at al-Taif,

1. Khadija, the Prophet's first wife owned and directed a financial business.

and dates and some cereals grew at the Oasis of Madinah; but Makkah was set in the midst of barren land. Government in Makkah was simple, direct and unorganized and had no civil or military bureaucracy."[1]

For scions of noble families in Makkah the only suitable vocation in life was commerce. Despite his high offices as keeper of the sacred well in Makkah and the Host of Pilgrims to Ka'abah, Abdul Muttalib's wealth had dwindled due to his exceeding munificence to his destitute kinsmen and helpless wayfarers. The young men of Hashim's clan had to fend for themselves in the competetive trading world of Makkah. They had little capital, but enormous managerial talent and vitality. Financiers and business magnates sought them as agents and executives to accompany their caravans to Syria and Yemen. The agents received shares in profit or a negotiated salary.

Financial integrity and acumen and a wholesome impressive personality is what a businessman looks for in an agent. And these qualities Abdullah possessed in abundance. The details of Abdullah's business enterprise are unrecorded. His last trading journey to Gaza, then part of Syria, has been mentioned by

1. Sydney Nettleton Fisher, *The Middle East : A History* (New York, 1959), pp. 22, 23.

tradition writers. Dr. Mohammad Hussain Haikal in his *Sirat al-Rasul* writes:

> "A short while after Amna's arrival in his home, Abdullah set out for Syria, a journey which lasted a few months. While returning he broke journey in Madinah to visit his relations there and relax. Meanwhile he was taken ill.[1]
>
> His companions of the caravan returned to Makkah and conveyed the news of his illness to Abdul Muttalib, who sent his eldest son Harith to look after Abdullah and bring him home after his recovery. On arrival in Madinah Harith learnt that one month after his stoppage in Madinah Abdullah had expired and his body had been interred there".

Ibn Sa'ad relates :

> "Amna had been pregnant eight months when Abdullah died. Abdullah bin Abdul Muttalib had accompanied a caravan of the Quresh on a trading journey to the famous city of Gaza in Syria. When the people of the caravan had finished their trading they returned and as they reached Madinah Abdullah fell ill.

---

1. Madinah's climate is damp and malarial—Many traditions speak of the Companions of the Holy Prophet (PBUH) lying with fever on their first arrival in Madinah.

So he said to his campanions", 'I am stopping in Madinah with my maternal cousins of the tribe of Idi bin al Nafar' Accord-ingly he stayed back in Madinah where he lay sick for a month. His colle-agues returned to Makkah and when Abdul Muttalib enquired from them the news of Abdullah they told him about his illness and his stopping in Madinah with his maternal cousins. On hearing this report Abdul Muttalib sent his eldest son Harith to fetch news of Abdullah. Upon his arrival in Madinah he learnt that Abdullah had already passed away and that his body had been buried in Dar-ul-Nabgha (the House of Nabgha). Nabgha, the owner of the house belonged to Beni Nagar. It was the same house which had a door on the leftside. Relatives described to Harith the sickness of Abdullah, his last days in Madinah, his will, his last moments and his funeral. Harith then carried the tragic news to his father Abdul Muttalib and the whole family went into mourning. The brothers and sisters of Abdullah were especially grief-stricken. The Holy Apostle was as yet in the womb of his mother. Abdullah was twenty-five years of age at the time of his death."[1]

1. Tabqat ibn Sa'ad Vol. I pp. 61-6

This tradition of Ibn Sa'ad about the circumstance of Abdullah's death and his age has found general acceptance among the scholars.[2]

2. (See for instance Abul Aa'la Maudoodi, *Sirat Sarwar-e-Alam,* (Lahore 78) P. 90.

AMNA'S ELEGY ON THE DEATH OF ABDULLAH

It was customary among Arab ladies of noble birth to compose elegies on the death of their relations expressing their sense of shock and highlighting the virtues and achievements of the departed soul.

The talented sisters of Abdullah must also have composed elegies on his death, but history has only preserved the elegy of his wife.

According to Ibni Saad Amna composed the following lines on her husband's death :

"Carry the news of the death of Ha-shim's son to the environs of Batha (Makkah).

Pay homage to him in the Ard-i-Ghama Gham (Madinah).

Fated Death beckoned him and he accepted the call.

Verily, there is no match for Hashim's family in the whole world.

Friends stricken with grief bore his pall to the Sepulchre."

In this Elegy Amna has paid just tribute to the patient nature of her husband. She has expressed her sense of "pride in the exalted position of Banu Hashim and their matchless qualities.

From the last hemistitch of the Elegy it can also be inferred that Abdullah was buried in Madinah with all marks of respect by a concourse of his friends and maternal relations.

Abdullah's Legacy

Ibn Sa'ad records that Abdullah left the following legacy for his son Muhammad (PBUH).

1. A female slave Umm-e-Aiman.

   Her title was Barkat. She looked after Muhammad (PBUH) in his childhood.

2. Five camels.
3. A few ewes.

Abdullah died young. For a man who had started his career but a short while before this is no mean achievement. Besides traditions speak of another wife that Abdullah had besides Amna and she must also have been provided for from his legacy.[1] Historical sources do not mention any son or daughter of Abdullah from the second wife. There is, therefore, strong evidence

1. Ibne-Ishaque, *Sirat Rasul Allah* trans. Gullaum (Oxford, 1955) p. 69.

that Muhammad (PBUH) was the only child of Abdullah. The Prophet had no step brother or sister.

A Note on Abdullah's Age.

Syed Amir Ali in his *Life of Muhammad,* gives 545 A.D, as the year of Abdullah's birth. The preponderance of opinion among the tradition writers is that Amna had been pregnant six or eight months when Abdullah died. The year of the Holy Prophets' birth is generally given as 570 or 571 A.D.[1]

Abdullah's age at the time of his death thus works out to be between 25 to 26 years which corresponds to Ibn Sa'ad's tradition.

---

1. T. Hughes, *Dictionary of Islam* p. 369.